Let's Learn About

Cats and Kittens

A Fun-to-Learn Activity Book

Written by
Suzanne Gruber

Illustrated by
Roseanna Cutrona-Pistolesi

Watermill Press

Cats of All Kinds

Cats come in many sizes and colors. There are little cats, big cats, white cats, black cats, striped cats, and more!

How many different kinds or "breeds" of cats can you find in this word-find puzzle? Use the word list below.

```
P E R S I A N S L B
J T V I Y W R H Z U
L W Q A L P E O B R
O L R M A N X R F M
N B W E J G L T H E
G C S S C D K H D S
H R J E Q Z Y A Q E
A B Y S S I N I A N
I X Z J A M C R D T
R H I M A L A Y A N
```

ABYSSINIAN
BURMESE
HIMALAYAN
LONGHAIR
MANX
PERSIAN
REX
SHORTHAIR
SIAMESE

What kind of cats grow on trees?

Answer: Pussy willows!

2

Siamese Twins

The Siamese was the royal cat of the kingdom of Siam, which is now called Thailand. Siamese cats have bright blue eyes and dark marks or "points."

Here are six Siamese cats. Can you find the two that are the same?

1.

2.

3.

4.

5.

6.

The Alley Cat

Domestic Shorthair cats, which are sometimes called "alley cats," are the best known and most popular of all the breeds. They have short, soft, shiny coats, which may be one color or a mixture of colors. Domestic Shorthair cats are faithful and lovable, but are also proud and fearless.

In the picture below, Allen the Alley Cat has met up with a very large mouse. What do you think they are saying? Fill in the cartoon with funny captions.

Calico Cat

Cats' coats have many different colors and markings. Some cats are all one color, some cats are striped, and some cats' coats are a mixture of colors. A cat that is "calico" has black, orange, yellow, and white patches all over it.

Color in this picture of a calico cat by following the numbers.

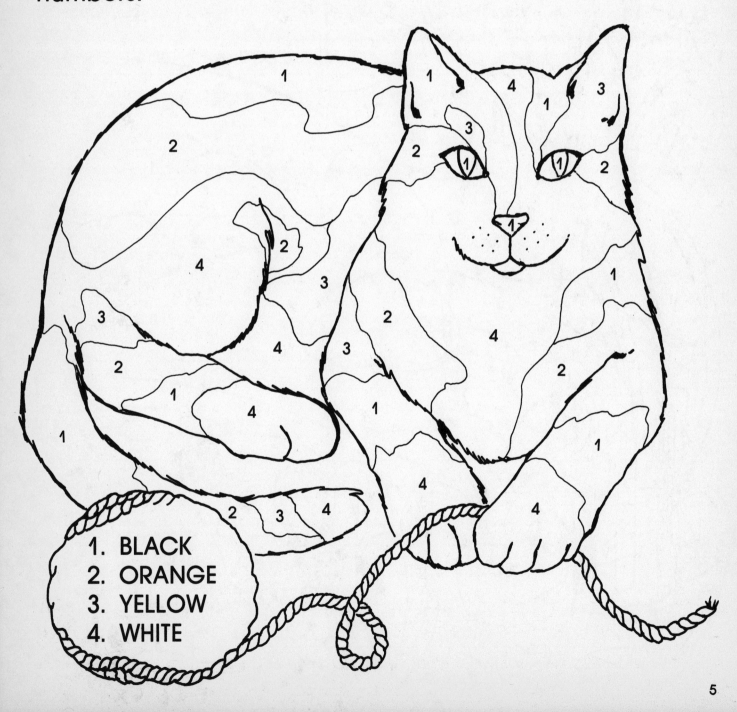

1. BLACK
2. ORANGE
3. YELLOW
4. WHITE

The Cat's Pajamas

When they are not playing and prowling, cats love to sleep. They especially like to take long "cat naps" in the sun. The mighty lion sometimes sleeps 19 hours a day!

It's bedtime for the lion family. How many sleeping lions can you find in this picture? Color them.

7

Wild Cats

Did you know that lions, tigers, and pet cats are all closely related? Many different kinds of animals belong to the cat or "feline" family. Some are tame and some are wild.

There are ten kinds of wild cats in this word-find puzzle. How many can you find? Use the word list below to help you.

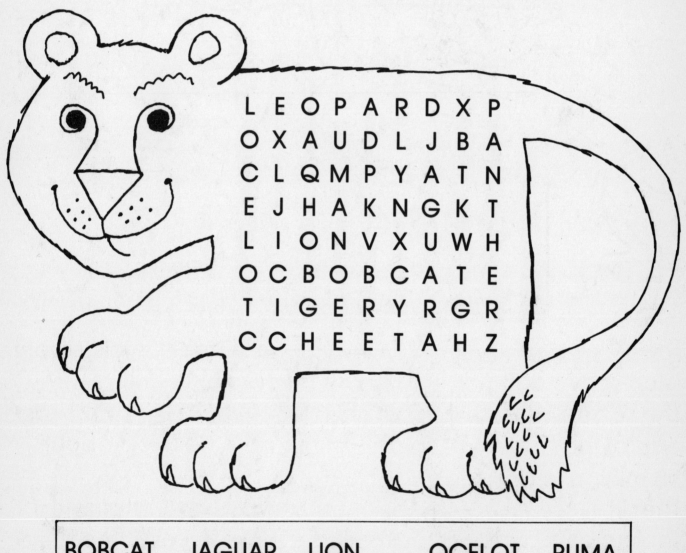

```
L E O P A R D X P
O X A U D L J B A
C L Q M P Y A T N
E J H A K N G K T
L I O N V X U W H
O C B O B C A T E
T I G E R Y R G R
C C H E E T A H Z
```

| BOBCAT | JAGUAR | LION | OCELOT | PUMA |
| CHEETAH | LEOPARD | LYNX | PANTHER | TIGER |

What do you call a dishonest cat?

Answer: A cheetah!

8

Facts On Cats

Cats are lots of fun to learn about! Did you know that the Manx is the only cat born without a tail?

There are more facts about cats below. But part of the sentences are in secret code! Use the secret decoder key to finish each fun-fact sentence.

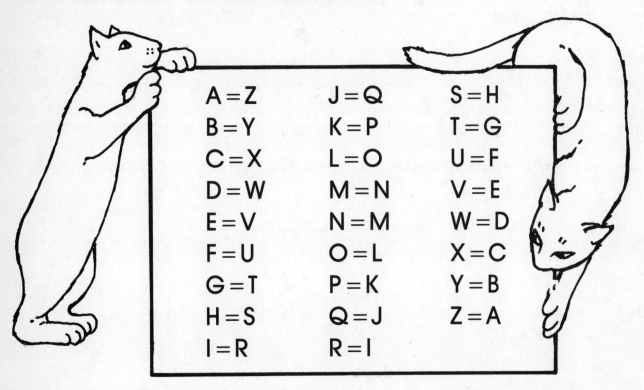

A = Z	J = Q	S = H
B = Y	K = P	T = G
C = X	L = O	U = F
D = W	M = N	V = E
E = V	N = M	W = D
F = U	O = L	X = C
G = T	P = K	Y = B
H = S	Q = J	Z = A
I = R	R = I	

1. The ——————————— ———————— cat has a thick, silvery,
   I F H H R Z M   Y O F V
   blue-gray coat. This kind of cat is very rare.

2. The saber-toothed tiger, or the ————————————————, was
   H N R O L W L M
   one of the most famous cats of the past. He lived about
   40 million years ago.

3. The —————————————————— cat may have originated
   Z Y B H H R M R Z M
   in Ancient Egypt. This cat's fur is "ticked," which means
   that each hair is marked with several different colors.

4. A newer breed of cat is the ————— . He has a very soft,
   I V C
   short and curly coat.

9

Feline Fun

Do you like crossword puzzles? Here is one all about cats. Read the clues below and fill in the blanks. Use the word list below to help you. Number 1 Across is done for you.

ACROSS

1. Long hairs that help cats feel their way.
3. A cat's sharp "fingernails."
5. The sound a cat makes.
6. Nice to look at, adorable.
8. Cats see very well with these.

DOWN

2. Black cats prowl on this spooky day.
4. A baby cat.
5. Cats like to chase these small animals.
7. A tame animal that you keep at home is called a _____ .

claws	Halloween	mice
cute	kitten	pet
eyes	meow	whiskers

WHISKERS

Cat In The Bag

Some cats can be very mischievous. They like to frolic and play games.

Cathy Cat is looking for her friend, Katy Kitty. Katy is hiding from Cathy in one of the bags below. She is hiding in the bag with the homonyms written on it. Homonyms are words that **sound** exactly the same, but have different meanings. Do you know which bag Katy is hiding in?

CAT
COAT

MAT
BAT

TALE
TAIL

LOOK
SEE

FULL
EMPTY

Nine Lives

There are many strange beliefs or "superstitions" about cats. Long ago, it was thought that cats were demons who helped witches. Even today, some people think that cats live nine lives, and that a black cat crossing your path means bad luck!

This little black cat got stuck on the roof of a spooky haunted house! Can you get him down, by helping him get through the maze?

Catnip

Most adult cats need only two meals a day to stay healthy and happy. But large cats, active cats, and kittens usually need three meals a day.

Cats eat many different kinds of food. Unscramble the words in the sentences below to find out what foods they like best.

<u>KMLI</u>   comes from a cow.   _____

<u>HFSI</u>   swim in lakes and oceans.   _____

<u>IKCNEHC</u>   is a bird that says "cluck."   _____

<u>MABUGRHER</u>   is ground beef.   _____

<u>EESCHE</u>   is a food that mice like to eat, too!   _____

Beans, peas, and corn are all <u>SEBVGETALE.</u>   _____

What do cats put on their hamburgers?

Answer: Cat-sup!

Cat Got Your Tongue?

Cats make certain sounds that no other animals make. House cats purr, especially when they are happy, and most wild cats let out loud roars.

The cats below have forgotten what to say! You can help them by filling in the blanks. Write the word "roar" next to each cat that roars. Write the word "purr" next to each cat that purrs.

Persian Puzzler

Persian cats have long, fluffy fur. Their beautiful coats can grow up to 5 inches long! Persians need lots of brushing and care to keep them looking nice.

This Persian cat's fur is all tangled! Can you find your way through the fur maze?

Start

Finish

The Owl and the Pussy-cat

Have you ever heard the story of the Owl and the Pussy-cat? Here is part of the funny poem:

> The Owl and the Pussy-cat went to sea
>   In a beautiful pea-green boat.
> They took some honey, and plenty
>   of money
> Wrapped up in a five-pound note.

There are ten things wrong with this picture of the Owl and the Pussy-cat. Can you find them all? Circle them.

A Thirsty Cat Riddle

What is a cat that drinks lemonade? To find out, cross out the word "lemonade" hidden in the three words below. The first letter is done for you.

LAE   SMOOUNR   APDUSES !

_____   _____   _____

Now color this picture.

Famous Cats

How many famous cats do you know? There are eight famous cats hiding in this word-find puzzle. See if you can find them all. For help, use the word list below.

```
H E A T H C L I F F F
D S B K Y W O Q E W
A Y G A R F I E L D
Q L Z M V J P Z I L
G V T O P C A T X K
R E L R Q G H J N T
W S V R C P S Q T O
Z T Y I D Y W J G M
K E M S B C M L B X
U R K R A Z Y K A T
```

Felix	Krazy Kat	Tom (Jerry's friend)
Garfield	Morris	Top Cat
Heathcliff	Sylvester	

Cat and Mouse

Most cats like to hunt. They have sharp eyes and can run very fast. The cheetah can run as fast as 60 miles an hour! That is as fast as a car goes.

Pet cats love to chase mice. How many mice can you find hiding in this picture puzzle? Color them.

Purr-fect Fun!

Here is a puzzle to test your memory. To solve the riddle below, read the clues and fill in the missing letters. If you get stuck on some of the clues, you can go back in this book and find the answers.

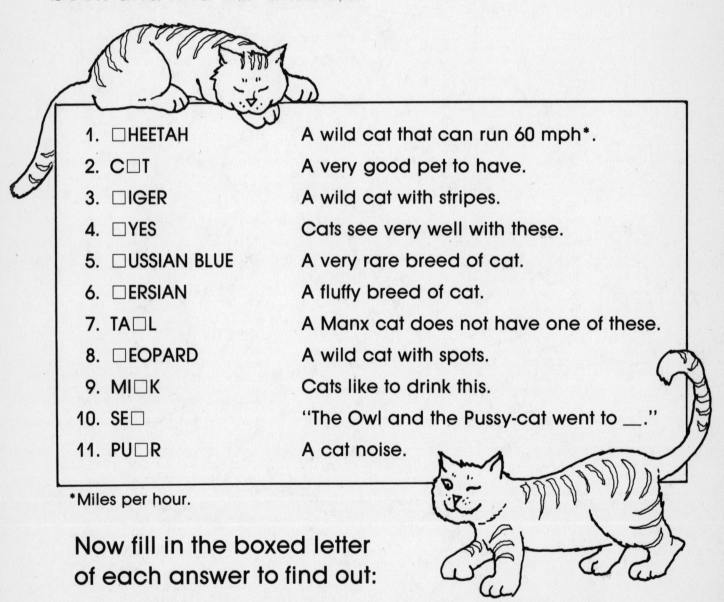

1. □HEETAH   A wild cat that can run 60 mph*.

2. C□T   A very good pet to have.

3. □IGER   A wild cat with stripes.

4. □YES   Cats see very well with these.

5. □USSIAN BLUE   A very rare breed of cat.

6. □ERSIAN   A fluffy breed of cat.

7. TA□L   A Manx cat does not have one of these.

8. □EOPARD   A wild cat with spots.

9. MI□K   Cats like to drink this.

10. SE□   "The Owl and the Pussy-cat went to __."

11. PU□R   A cat noise.

*Miles per hour.

Now fill in the boxed letter of each answer to find out:

WHAT DO YOU GET WHEN YOU CROSS A CAT WITH A BUG?

□ □ □ □ □ □ □ □ □ □ □

1. 2. 3. 4. 5. 6. 7. 8. 9. 10. 11.

Puss in Boots

Cats don't really wear boots, but this cat does!

Can you help him find his pair of matching boots? Just find the two boots with the numbers that add up to 100.

Time for Rhyme

A swimming cat could be called a "wet pet" and a grouchy cat could be called a "crabby tabby!"
Here are some clues with rhyming answers. Just read the clues, and unscramble the underlined words to find the rhyme.

1. An overweight feline is a <u>TFA ACT</u>. _ _ _ _   _ _ _

2. A nice-looking baby cat is a <u>PTYRET YTKIT</u>. _ _ _ _ _ _   _ _ _ _ _ _

3. A sad King of the Beasts is a <u>NYICR' IOLN</u>. _ _ _ _ _ _ _' _ _ _ _ _

4. An evil curse on a wild cat is a <u>NXLY INJX</u>. _ _ _ _ _   _ _ _ _ _

5. Baby cats' gloves are <u>TTKNIES' MNTSTIE</u>.
_ _ _ _ _ _ _ _' _ _ _ _ _ _ _ _

6. A wild cat sprinkled with a spice is a <u>PEPRPEDE OPELADR</u>. _ _ _ _ _ _ _ _   _ _ _ _ _ _ _ _

Kitten Kaboodle

Baby cats are called "kittens." These adorable furry babies love to cuddle and play games. Kittens grow very fast. By the time they are eight or nine weeks old, they are almost fully grown!

This little kitten is playing with a ball of yarn. Do you know which ball of yarn he is playing with? To find out, follow the line the kitten is holding.

1.

2.

3.

4.

Kitty Corner

Kittens need plenty of love and attention. You should feed your kitten two or three times a day and always give him fresh water. You should change your kitten's litter box every few days. And you should take your kitten to see a doctor for a check-up.

Here is a crossword puzzle about kittens. Read the clues below and then fill in the blanks. Number 1 Down is done for you. Use the word list below to help you.

ACROSS
3. Kittens love to drink this.
4. Never pull a cat's _____ !
6. Kittens are lots of _____ to play with.
7. The noise a kitten makes when you pet him.
9. Kittens need plenty of this.
10. What kittens grow up to be.

DOWN
1. A word to describe kittens.
2. Kittens like to play with balls of string or _____ .
5. Opposite of "big."
6. Soft, fuzzy hair.
8. Three little kittens _____ their mittens.

cats	little	milk	tail
fun	lost	playful	yarn
fur	love	purr	

The Kittens' Mittens

The three little kittens have lost their mittens! Help the kittens by finding their missing mittens in this picture. Draw a line from each hidden mitten to its owner.

Answer Page

Page 2   Cats of All Kinds

P	E	R	S	I	A	N	S	L	B
J	T	V	I	Y	W	R	H	Z	U
L	W	Q	A	L	P	E	O	B	R
O	L	R	M	A	N	X	R	F	M
N	B	W	E	J	G	L	T	H	E
G	C	S	S	C	D	K	H	D	S
H	R	J	E	Q	Z	Y	A	Q	E
A	B	Y	S	S	I	N	I	A	N
I	X	Z	J	A	M	C	R	D	T
R	H	I	M	A	L	A	Y	A	N

Page 3   Siamese Twins
           #3   #4

Pages 6 & 7   The Cat's Pajamas

       10 Sleeping lions , one is awake.

Page 8   Wild Cats

L	E	O	P	A	R	D	X	P
O	X	A	U	D	L	J	B	A
C	L	Q	M	P	Y	A	T	N
E	J	H	A	K	N	G	K	T
L	I	O	N	V	X	U	W	H
O	C	B	O	B	C	A	T	E
T	I	G	E	R	Y	R	G	R
C	C	H	E	E	T	A	H	Z

Page 9   Facts On Cats

     1. Russian Blue   3. Abyssinian
     2. Smilodon   4. Rex

Pages 10 & 11   Feline Fun

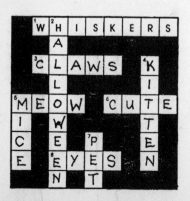

Page 12   Cat in the Bag
                   Tale-Tail

Page 13   Nine Lives

Page 14   Catnip
     MILK
     FISH
     CHICKEN
     HAMBURGER
     CHEESE
     VEGETABLES

Page 15   Cat Got Your Tongue?

     3 Large Cats Roar
     5 Small Cats Purr

Pages 16 & 17   Persian Puzzler

Answer Page

Pages 18 & 19

The Owl and the Pussy-cat

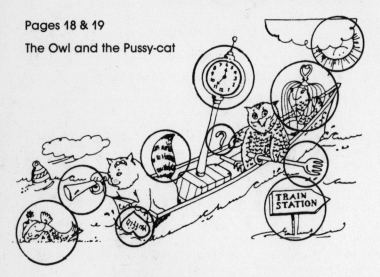

Page 20   A Thirsty Cat Riddle

A SOUR PUSS

Page 21   Famous Cats

Pages 22 & 23   Cat and Mouse

11 mice

Page 24   Purr-fect Fun!

1-CHEETAH	7-TAIL
2-CAT	8-LEOPARD
3-TIGER	9-MILK
4-EYES	10-SEA
5-RUSSIAN BLUE	11-PURR
6-PERSIAN	

CATERPILLAR

Page 25   Puss in Boots

$45 + 55 = 100$

Page 26   Time for Rhyme

1-FAT CAT
2-PRETTY KITTY
3-CRYIN' LION
4-LYNX JINX
5-KITTENS' MITTENS
6-PEPPERED LEOPARD

Page 27   Kitten Kaboodle   #4

Pages 28 & 29   Kitty Corner

Page 30   The Kittens' Lost Mittens